This Book Belongs To.....

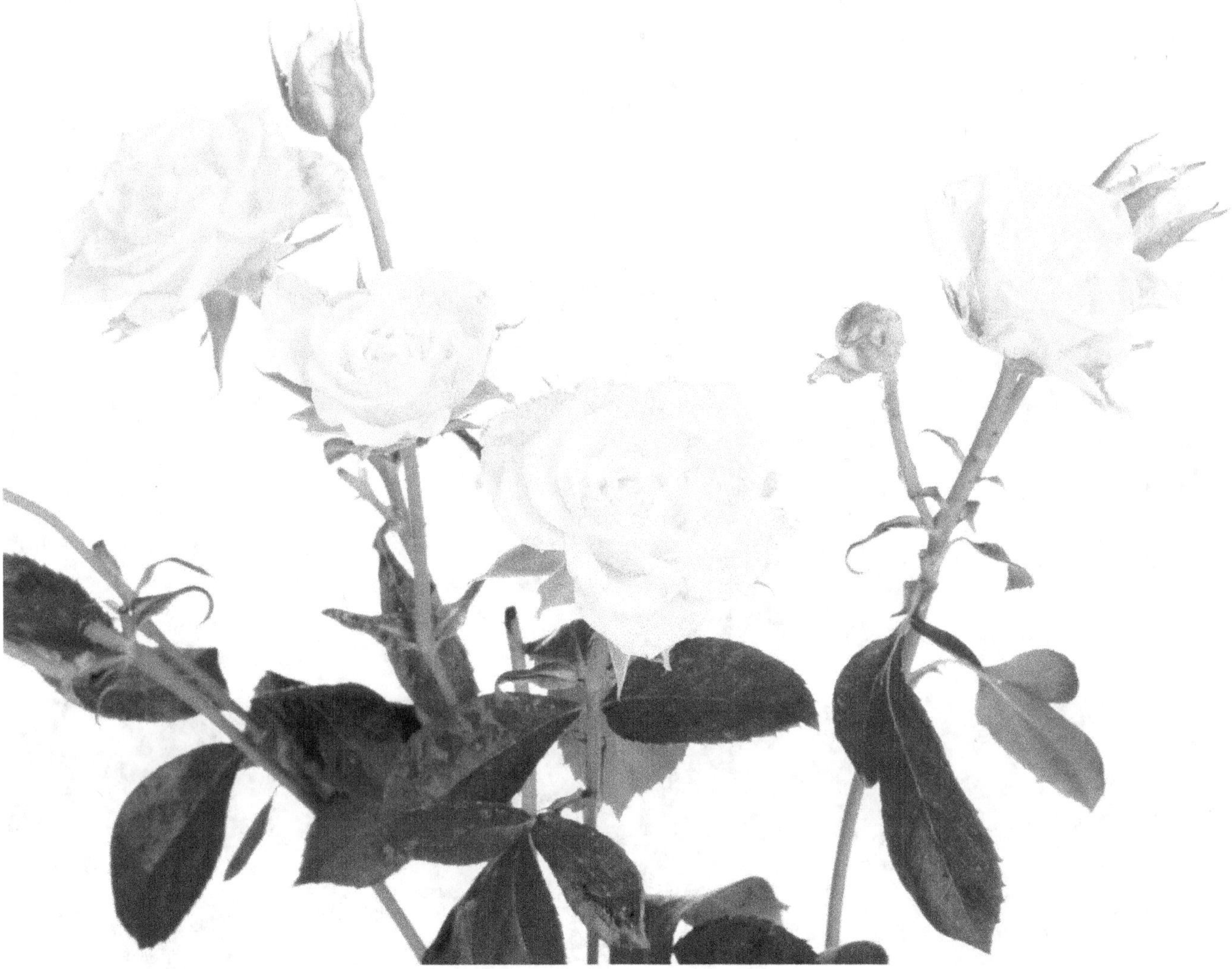

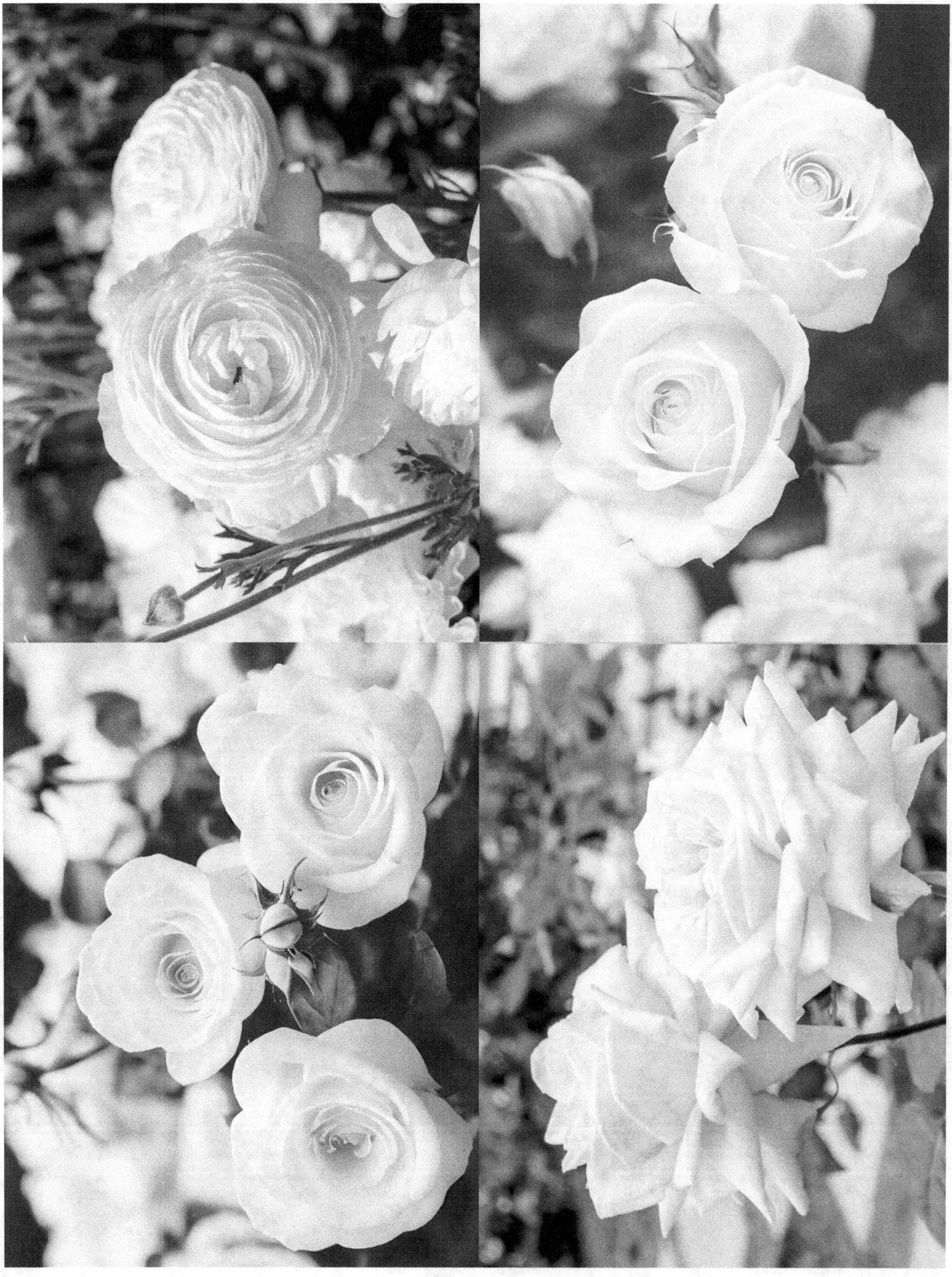

ROSE FLOWERS GRAYSCALE

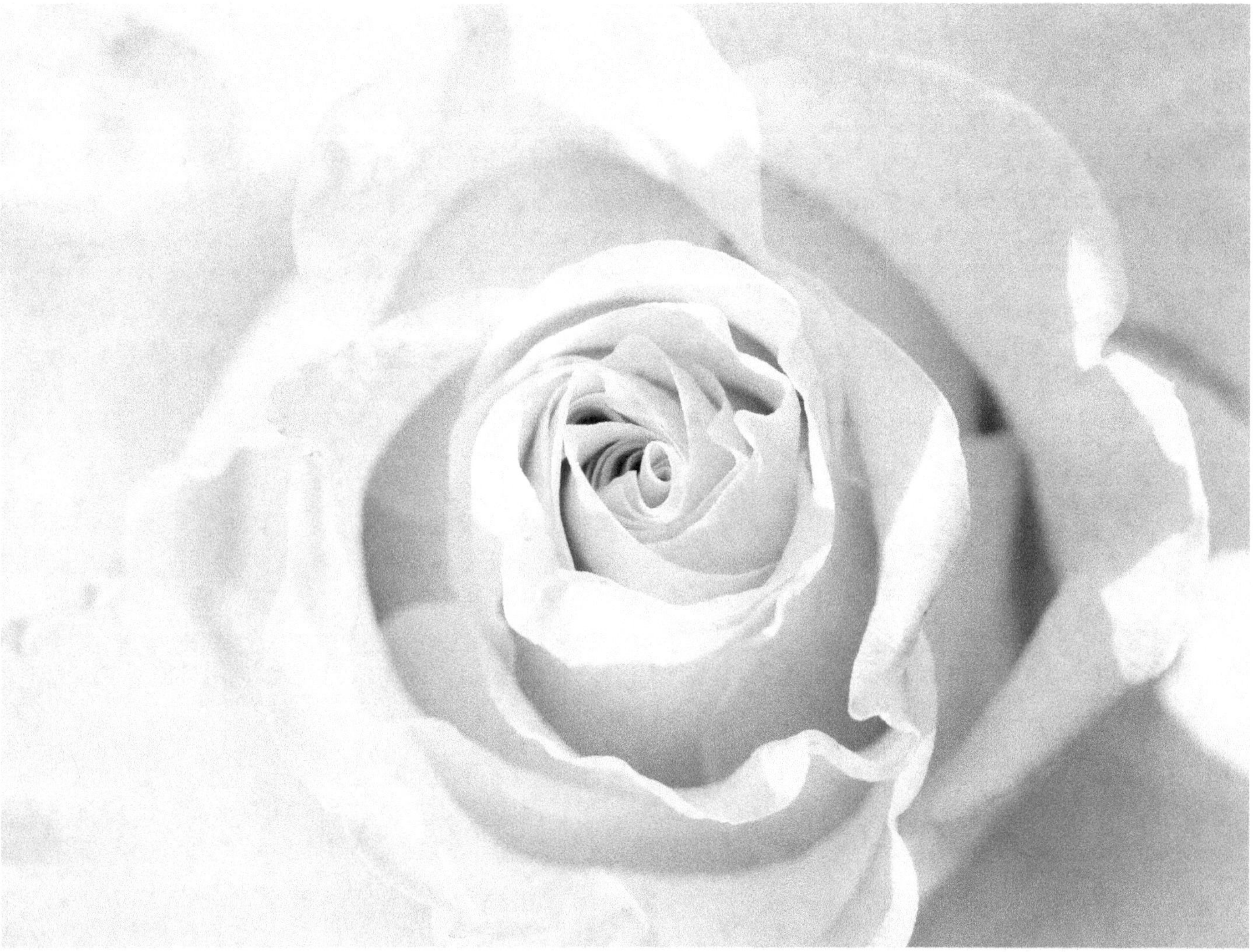

Copyright: Published in the United States
Published 2024
MOO MOO PINK

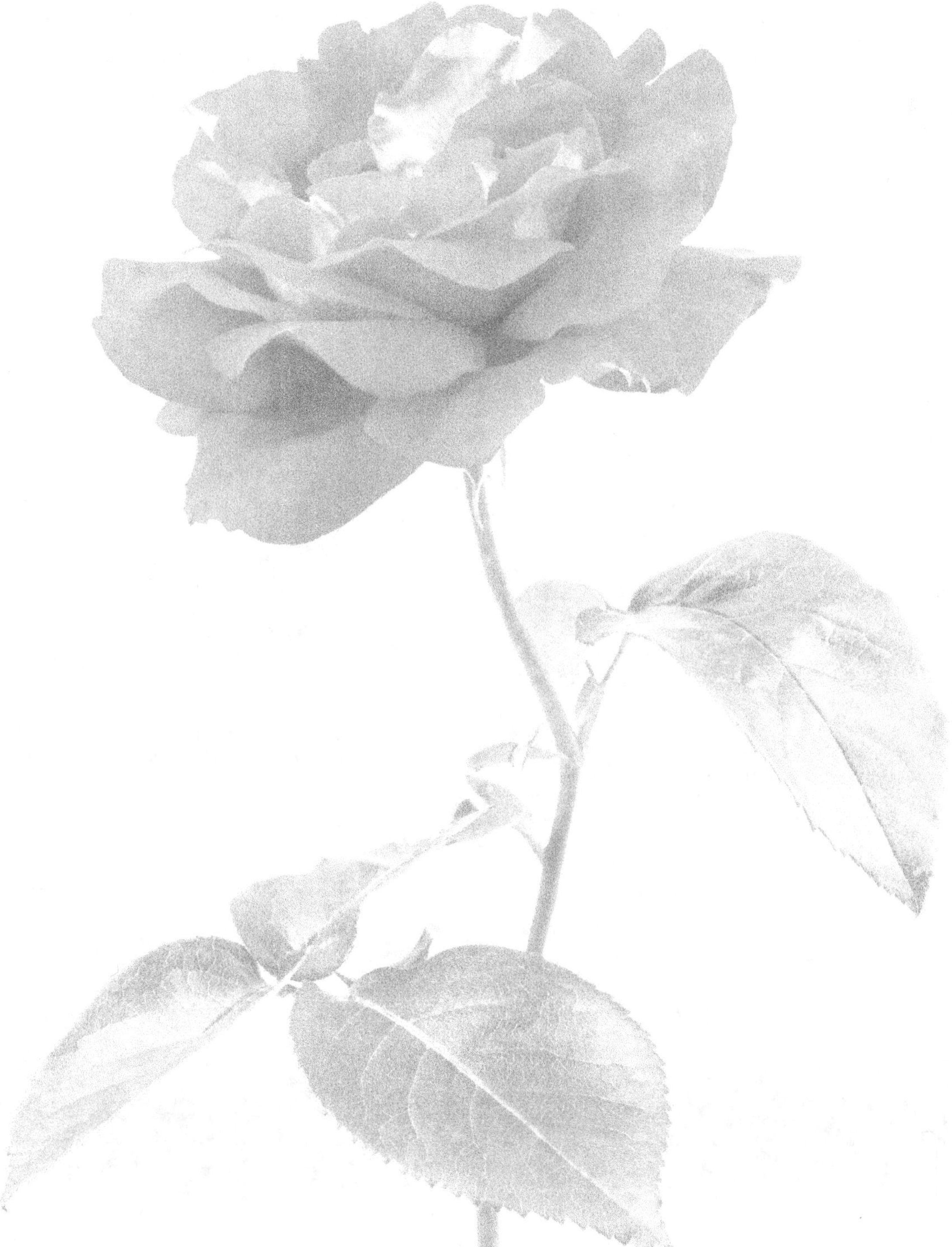

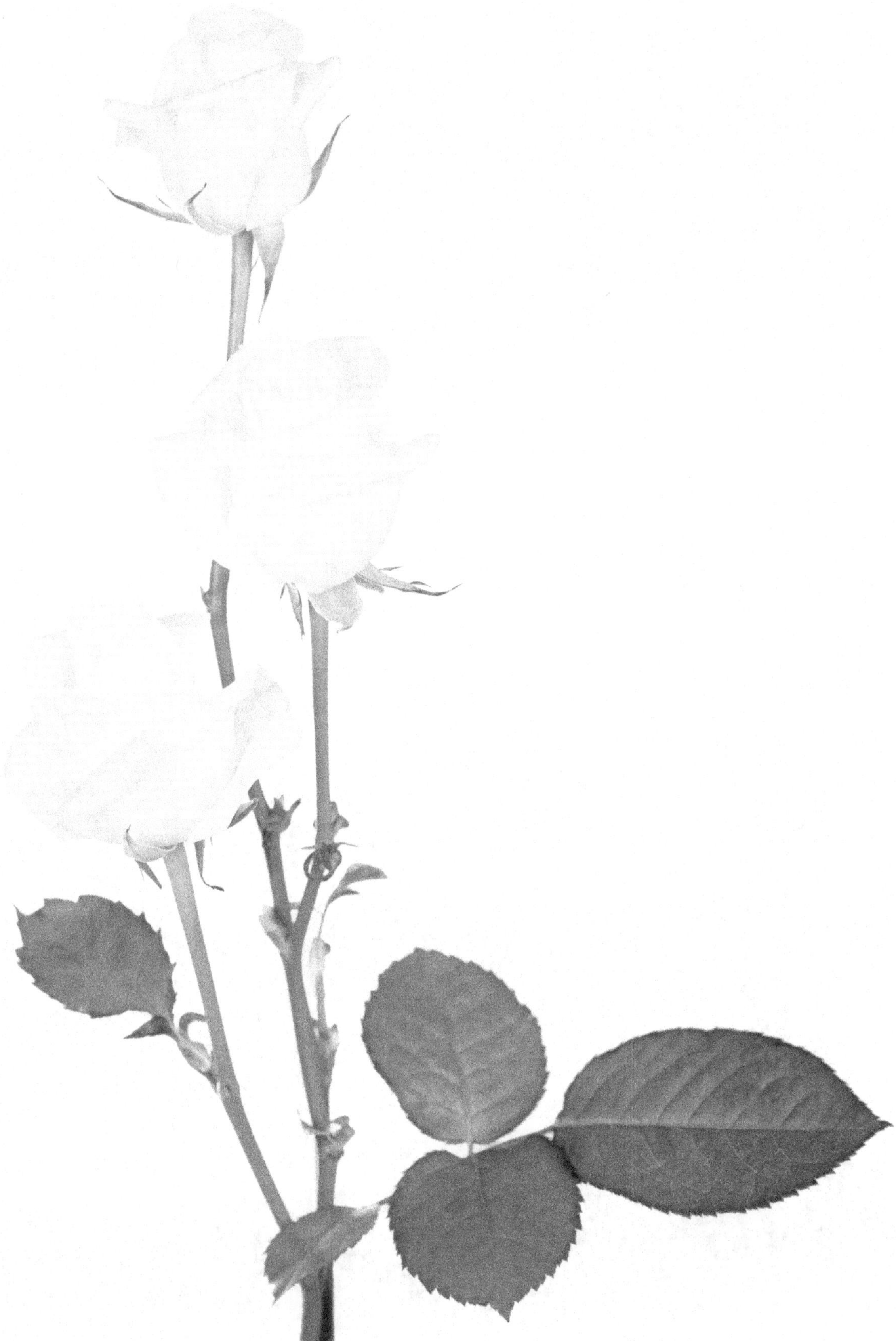

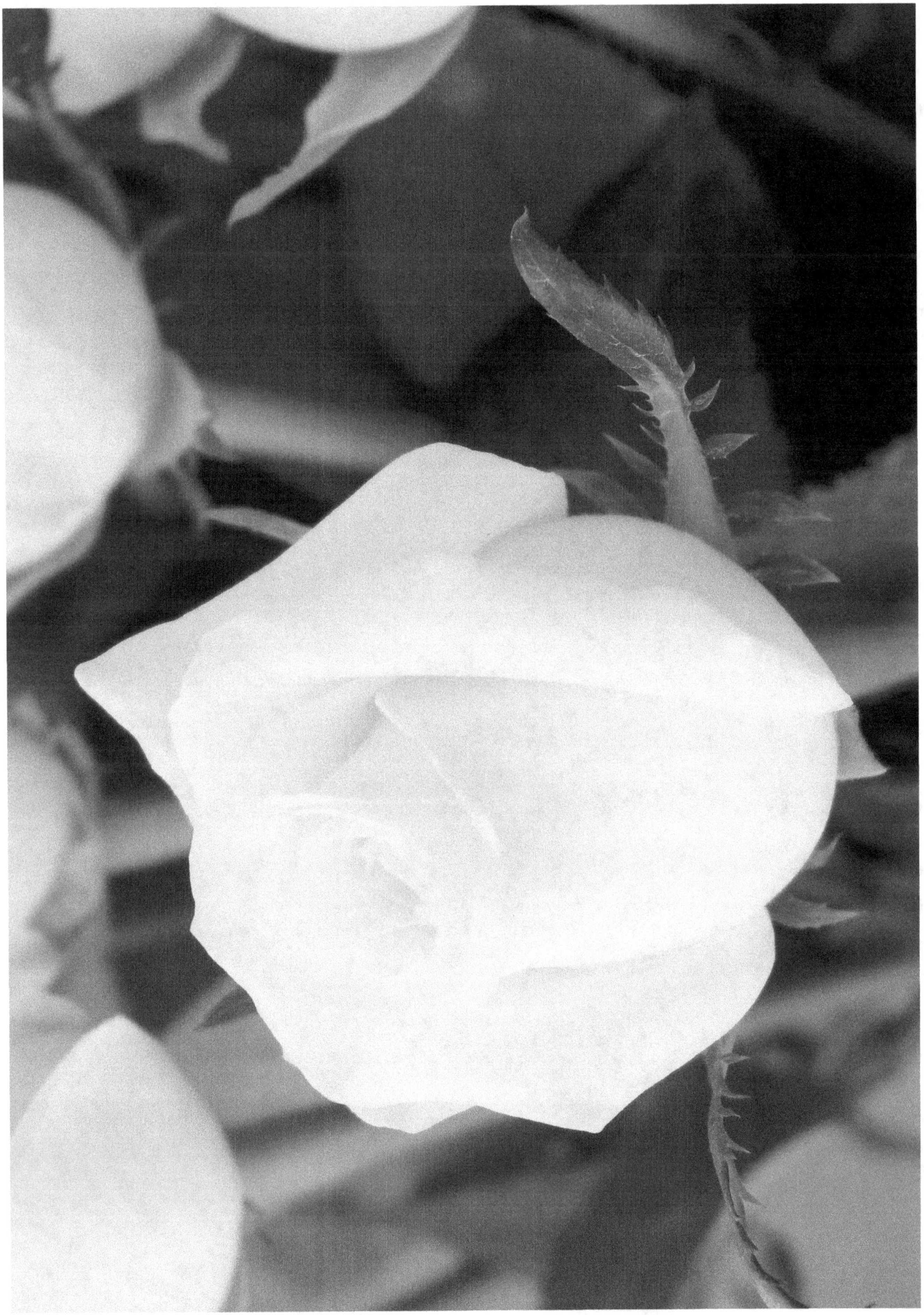

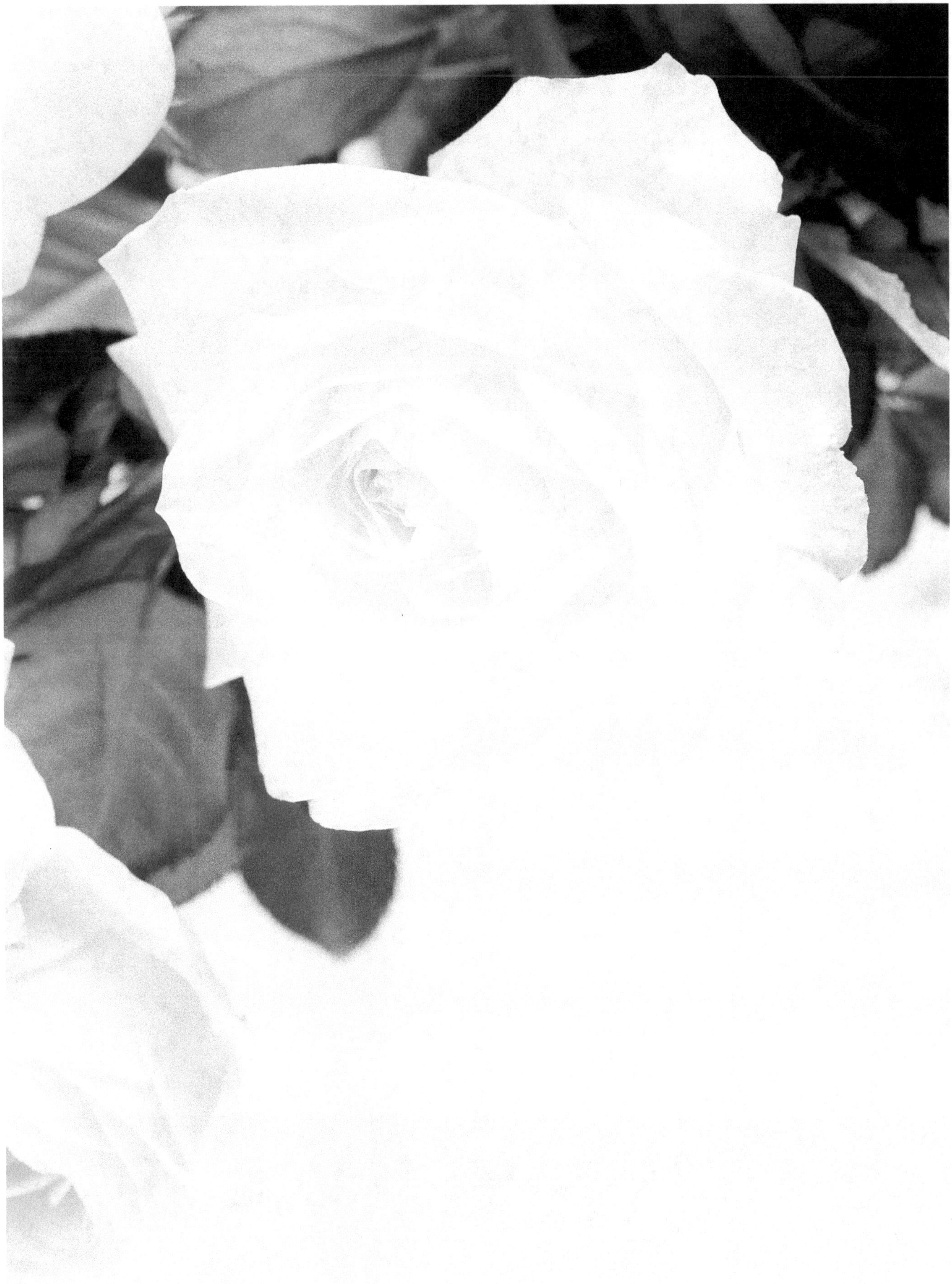

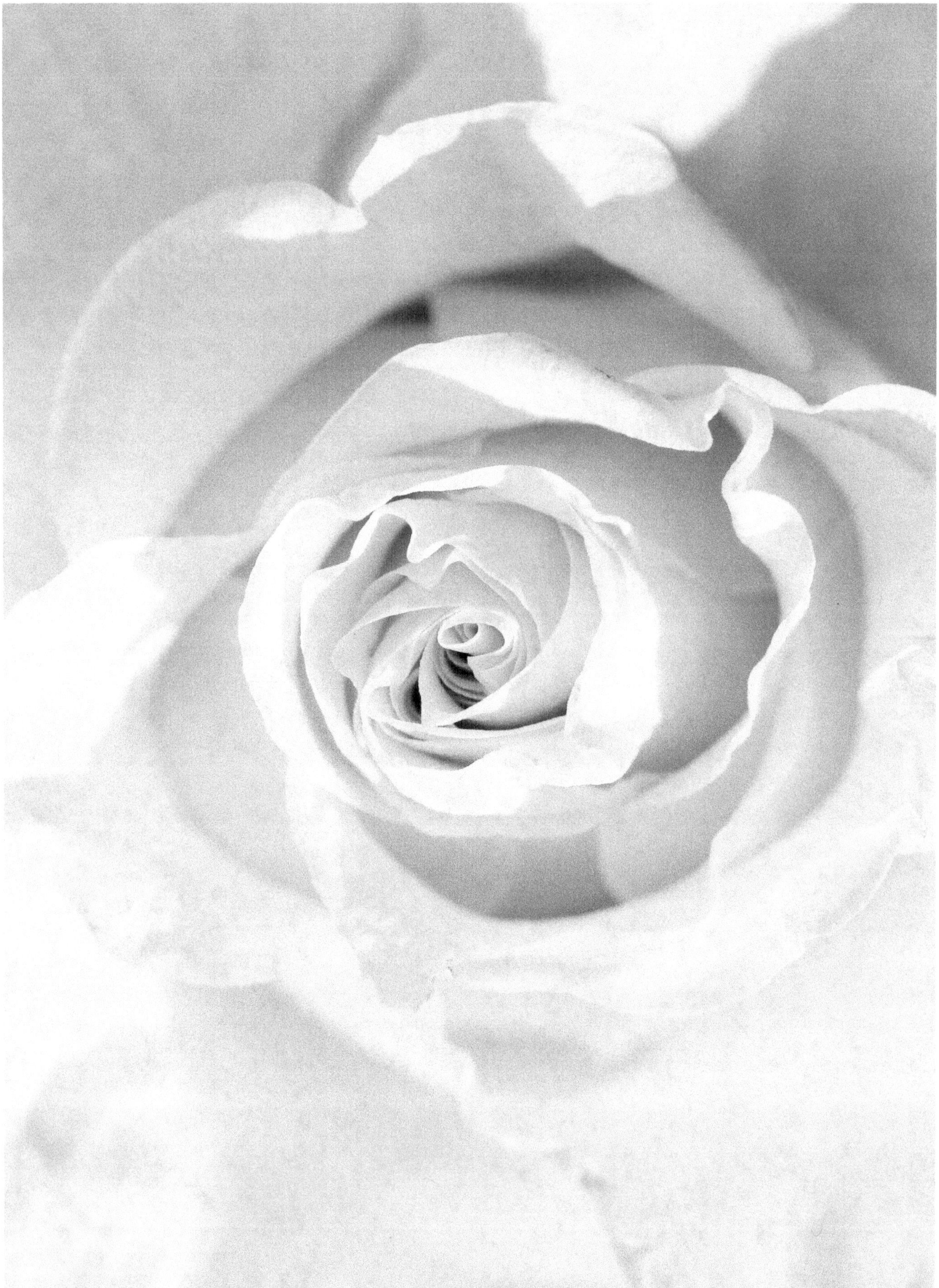

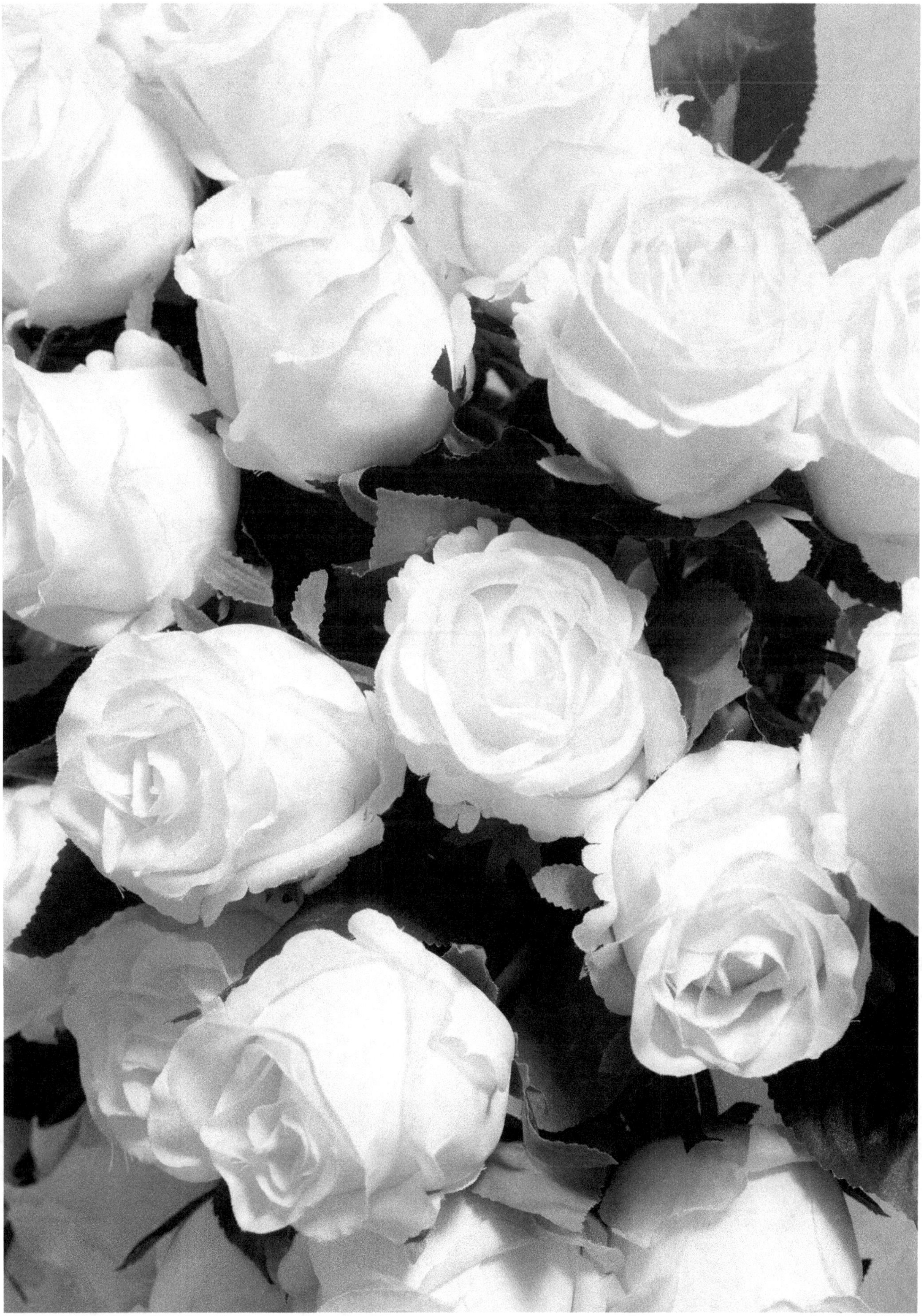

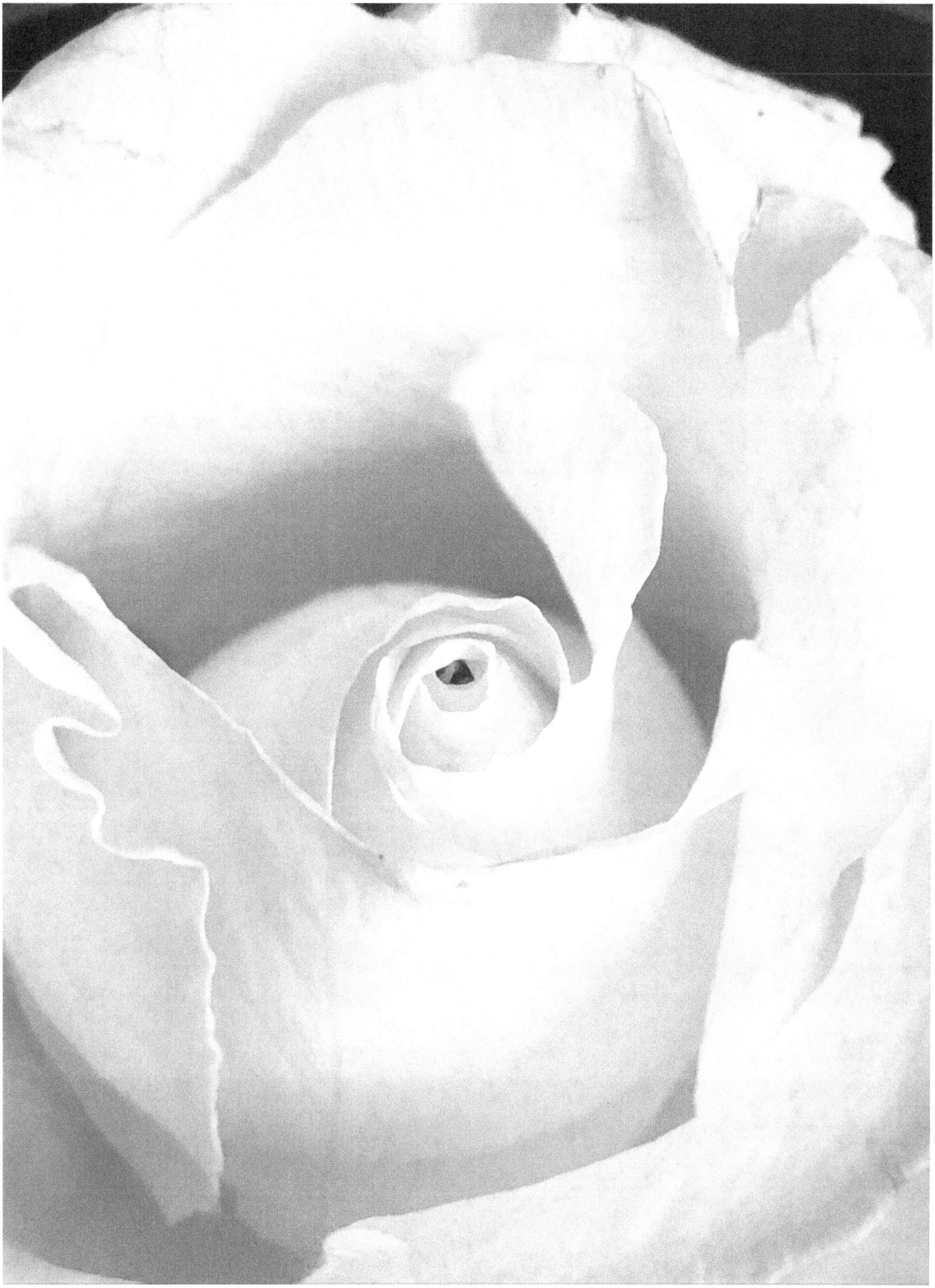

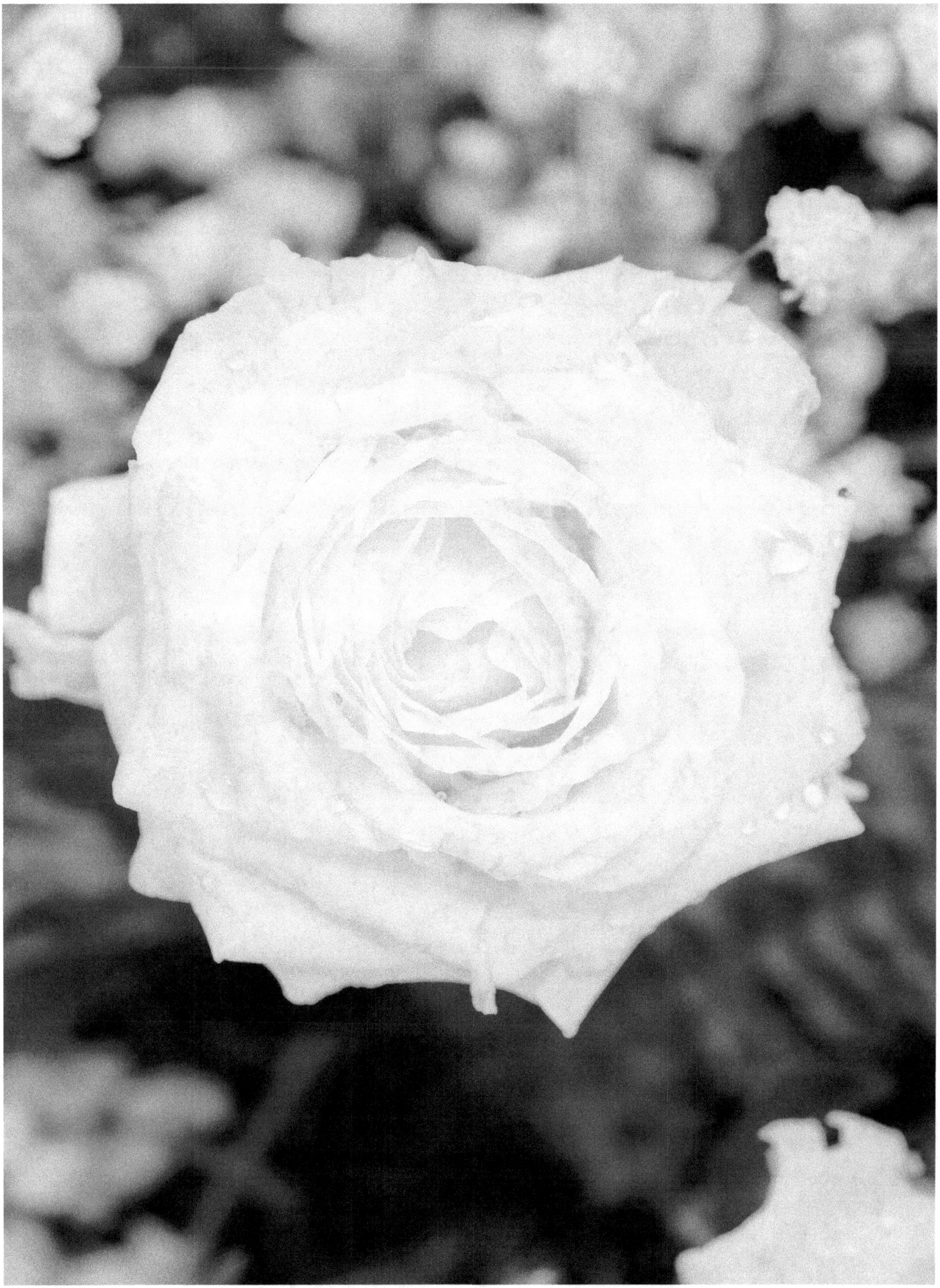

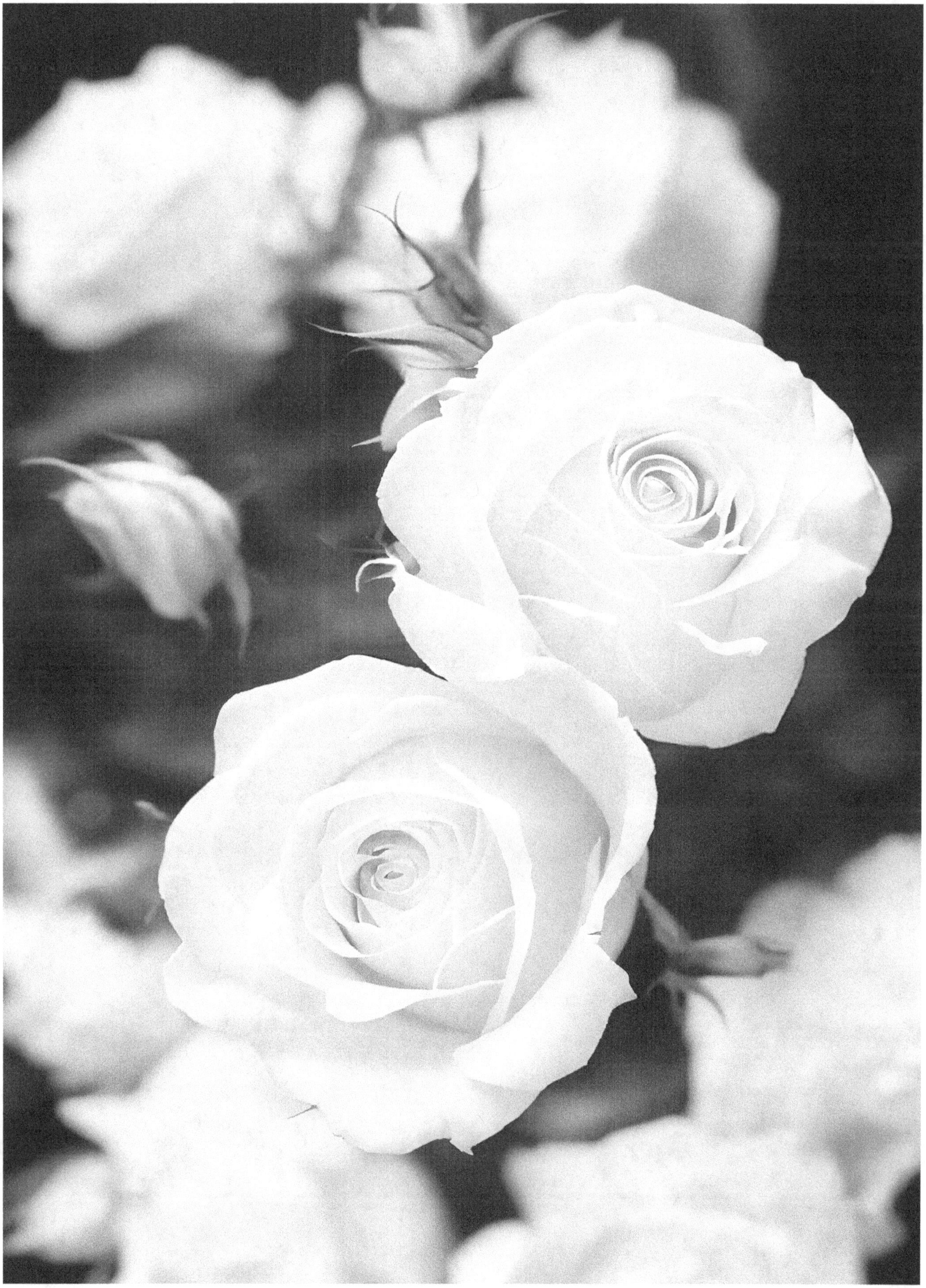

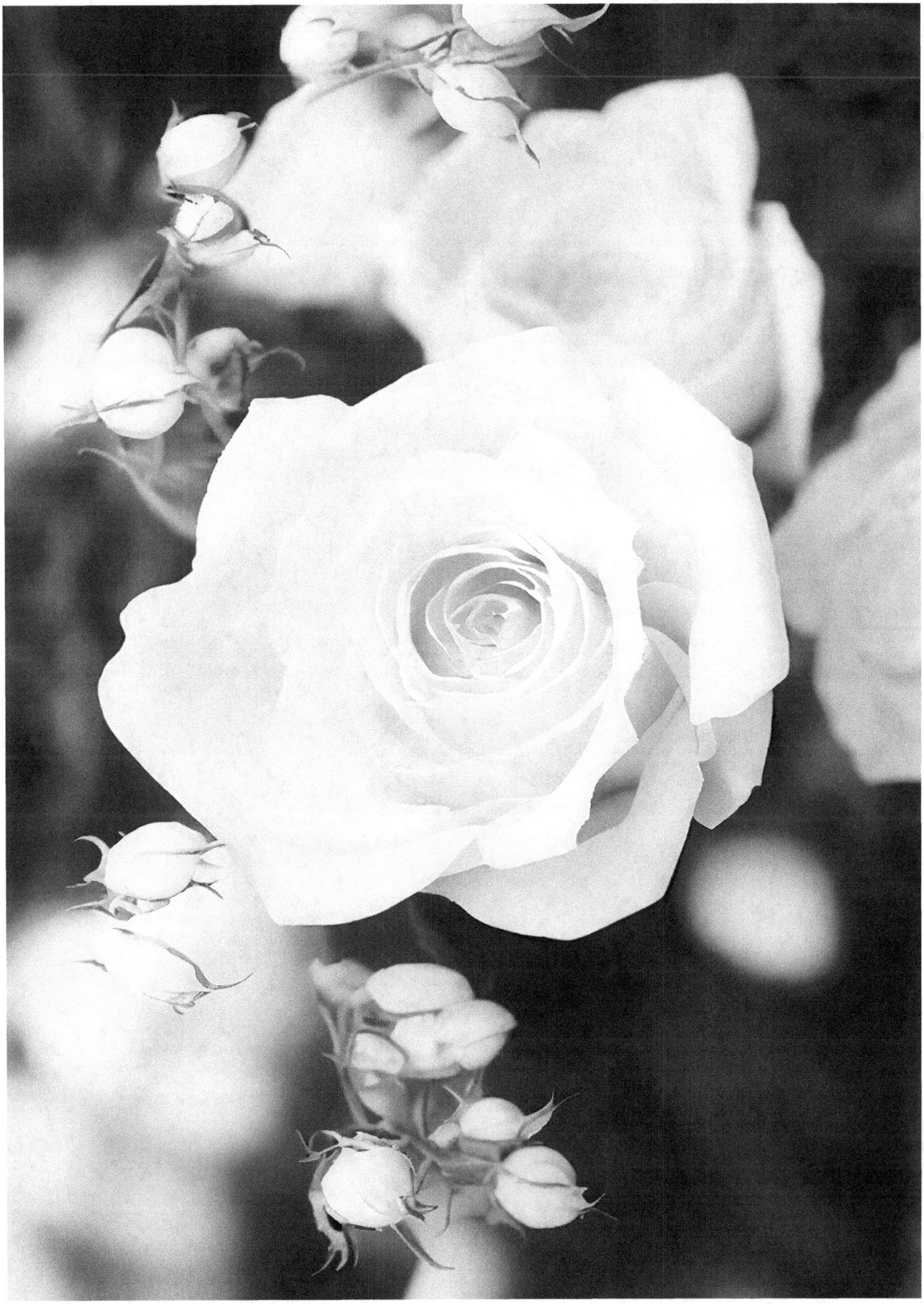

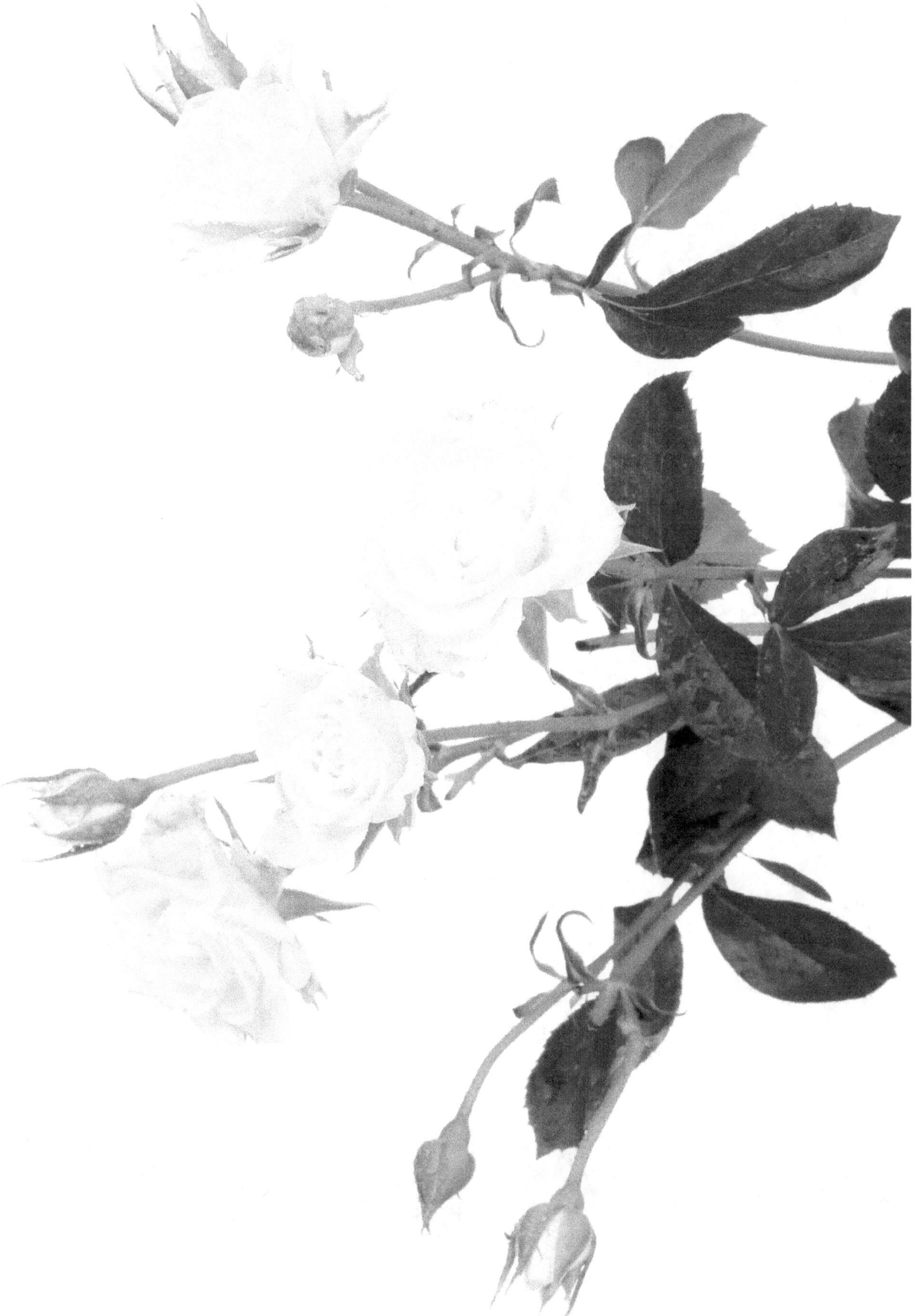

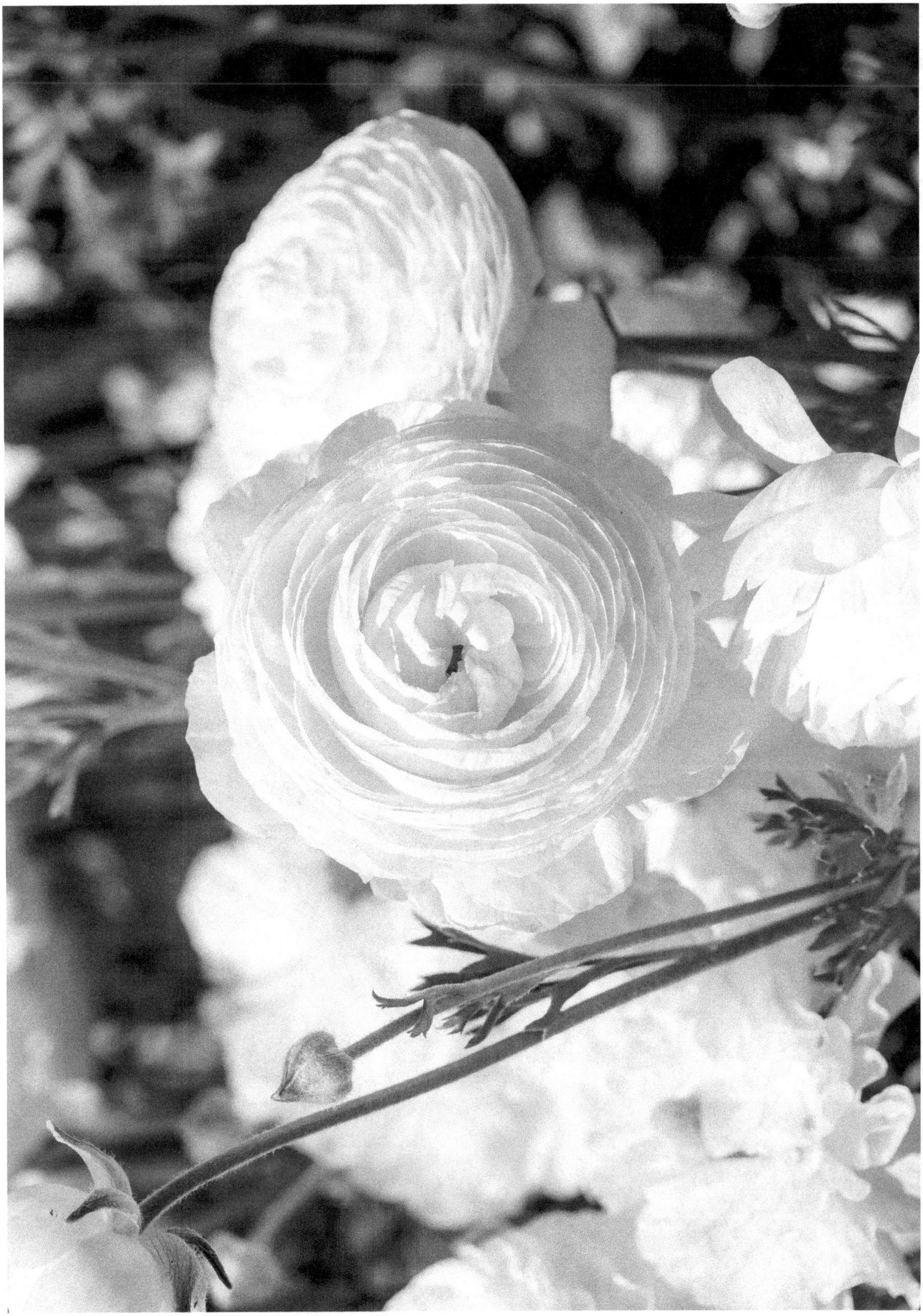

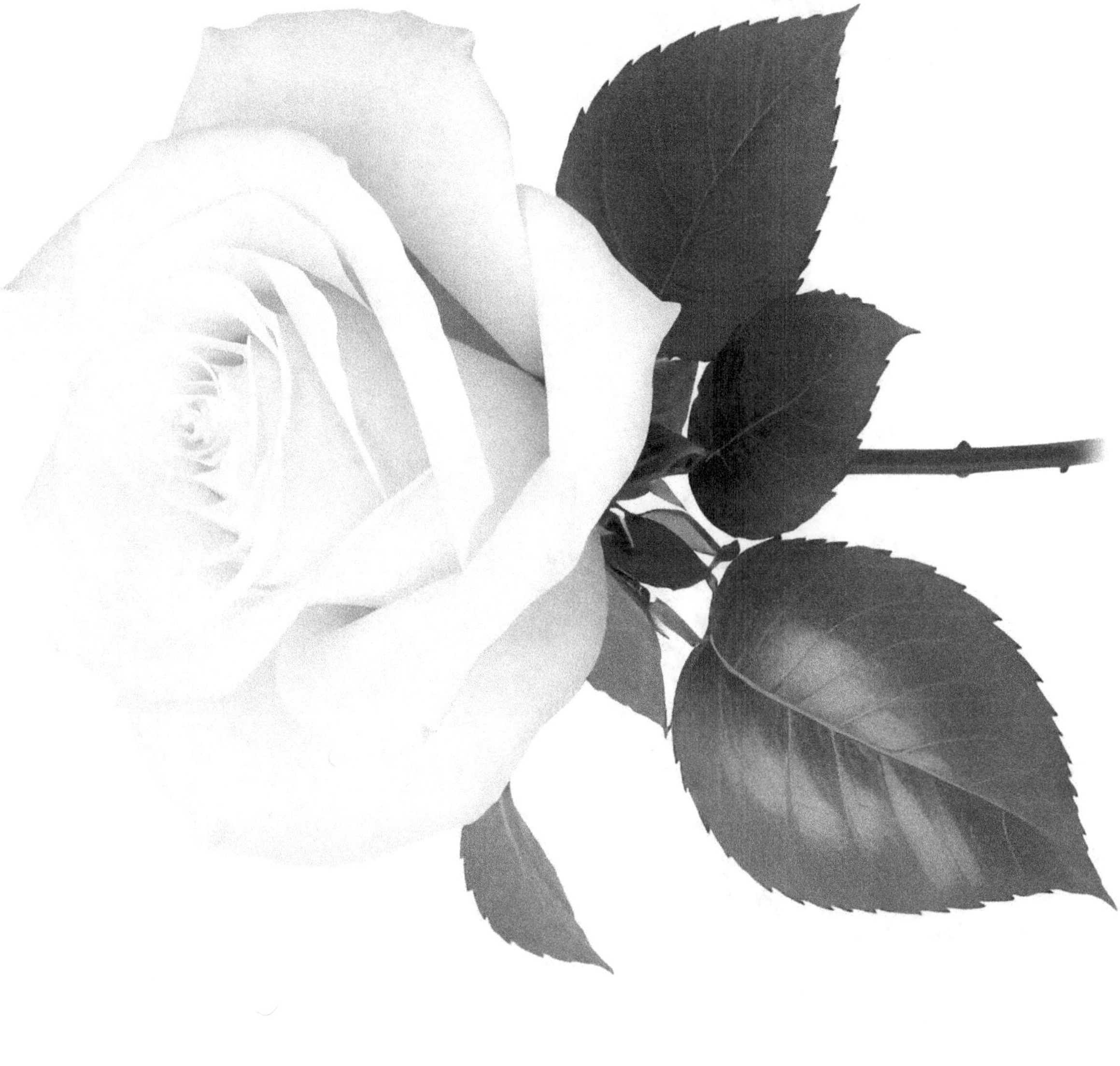

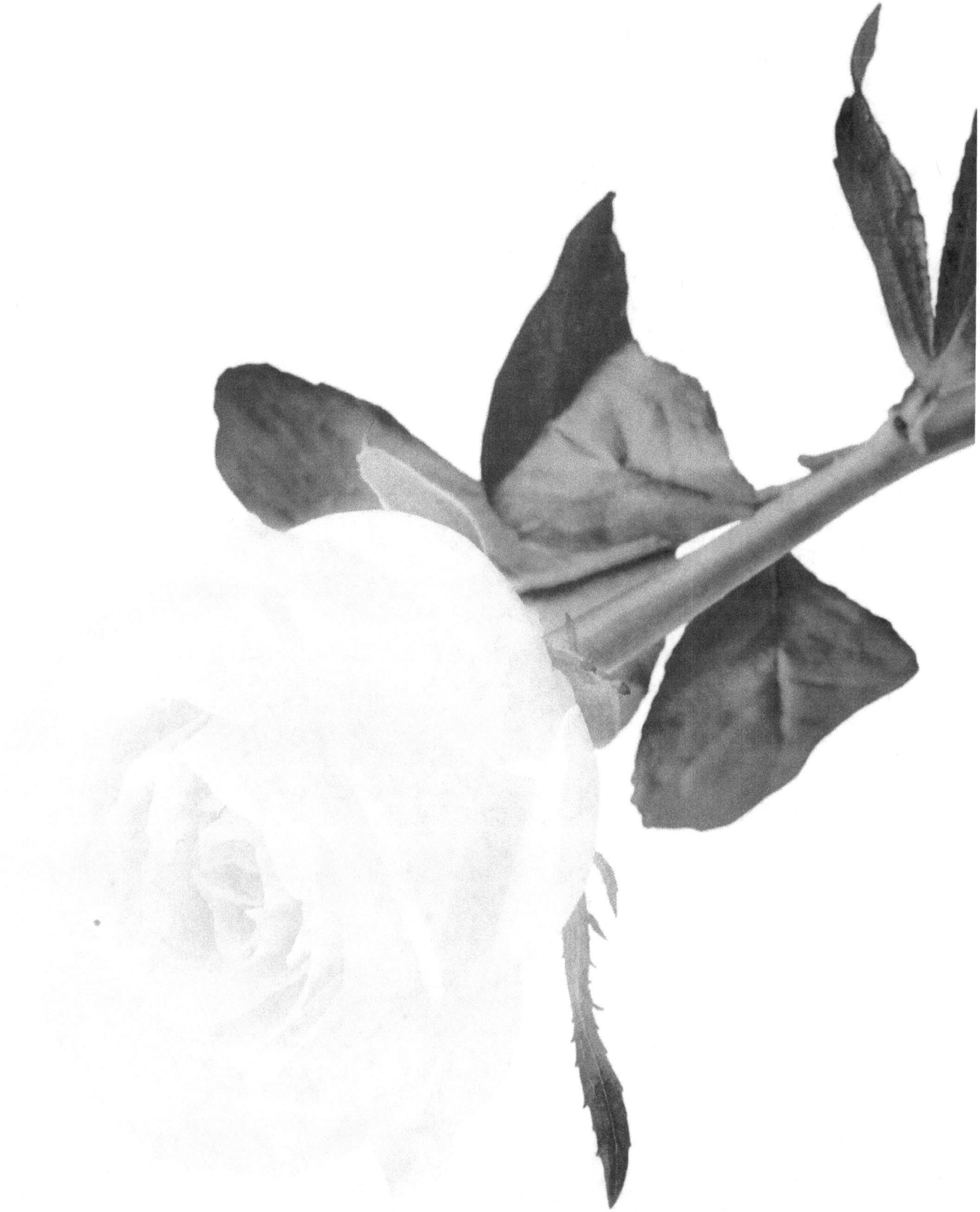

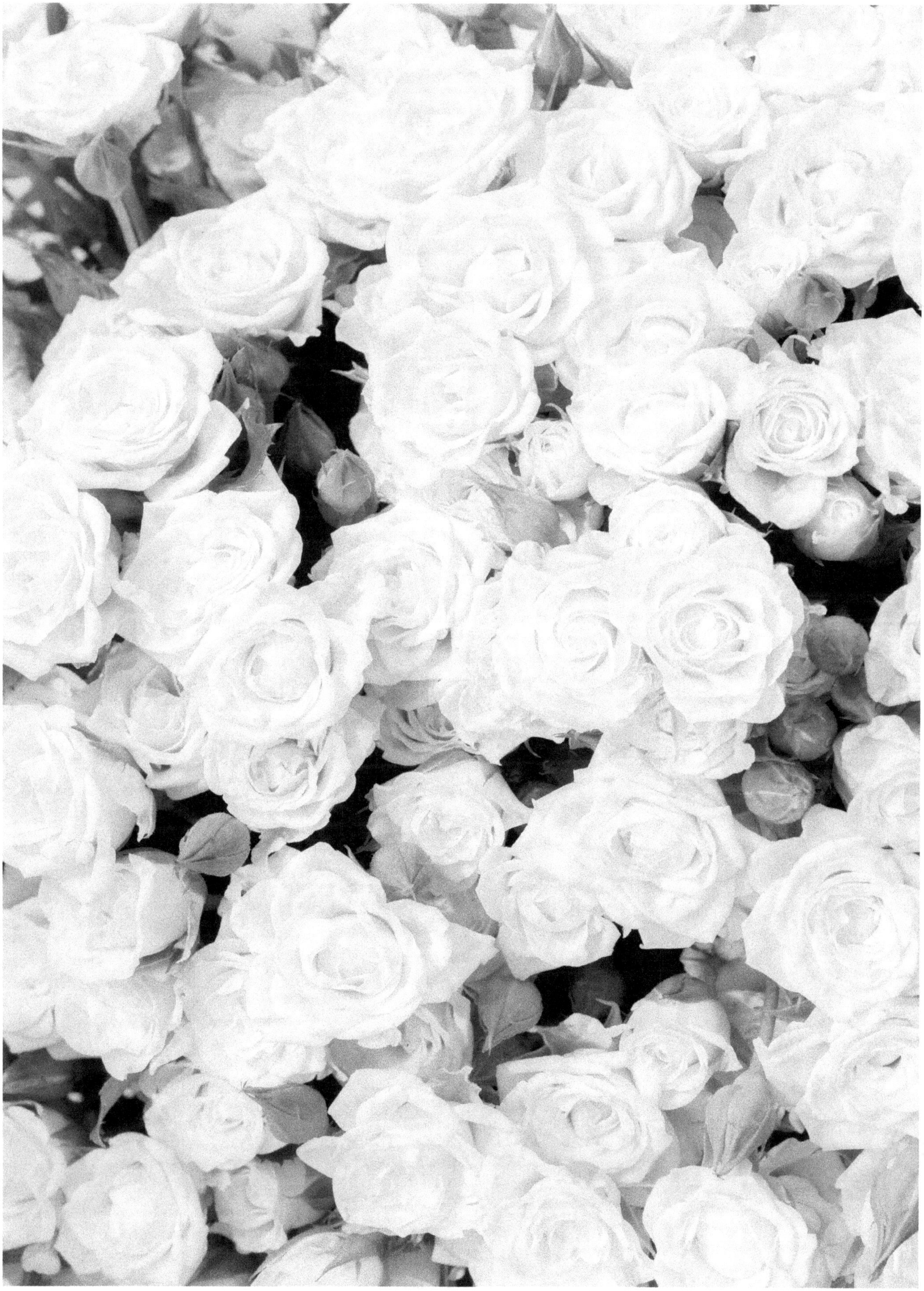

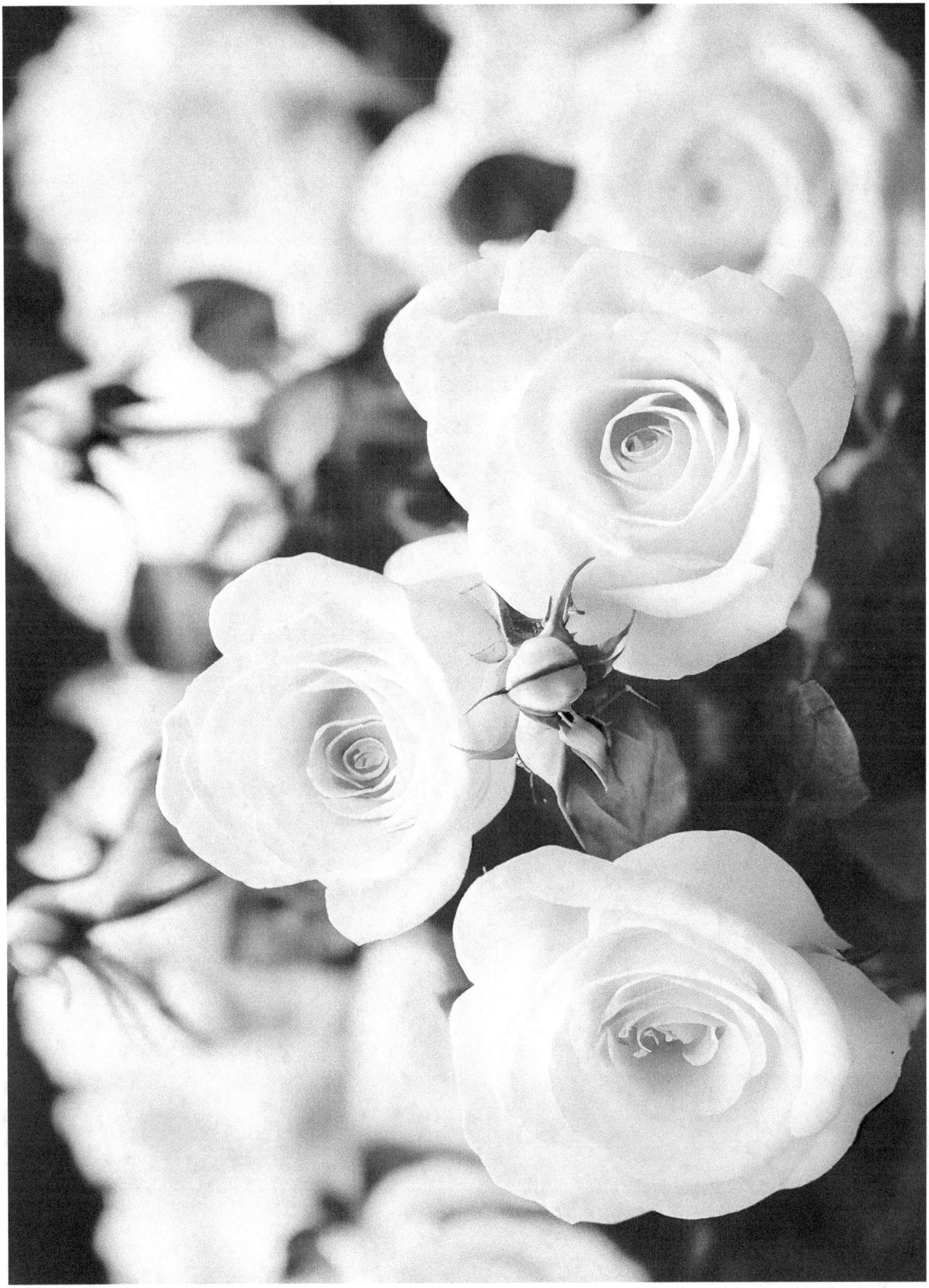

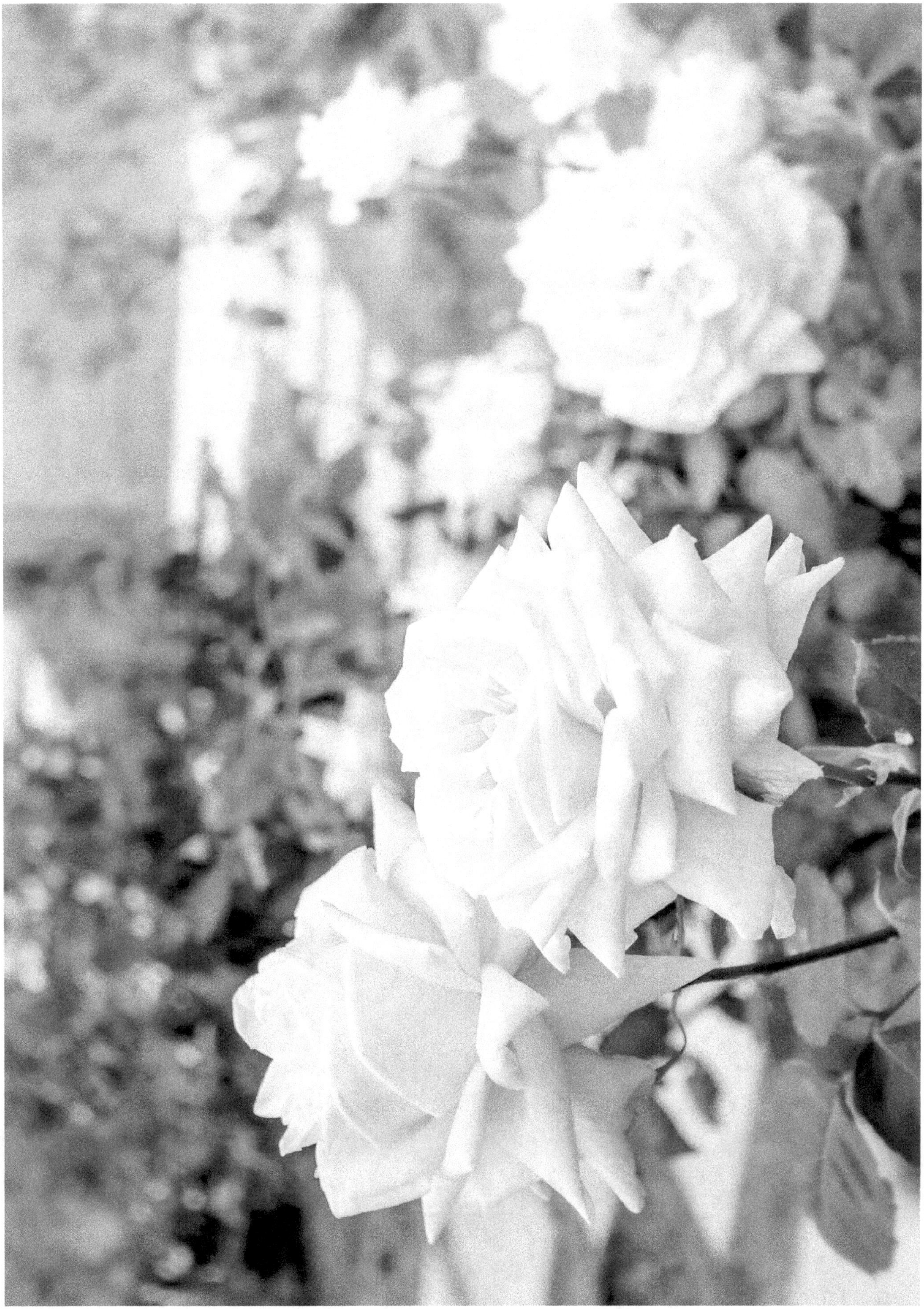

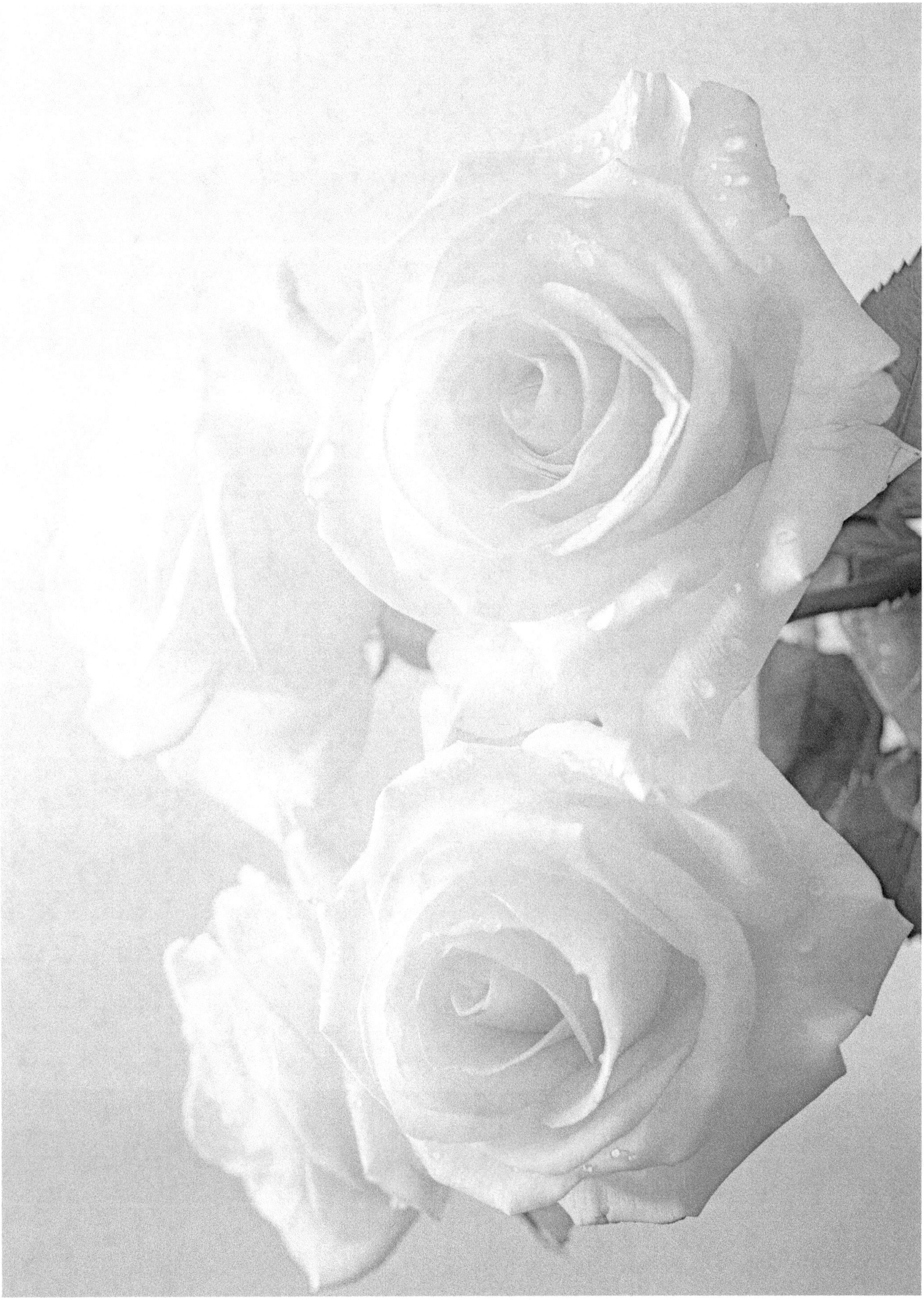

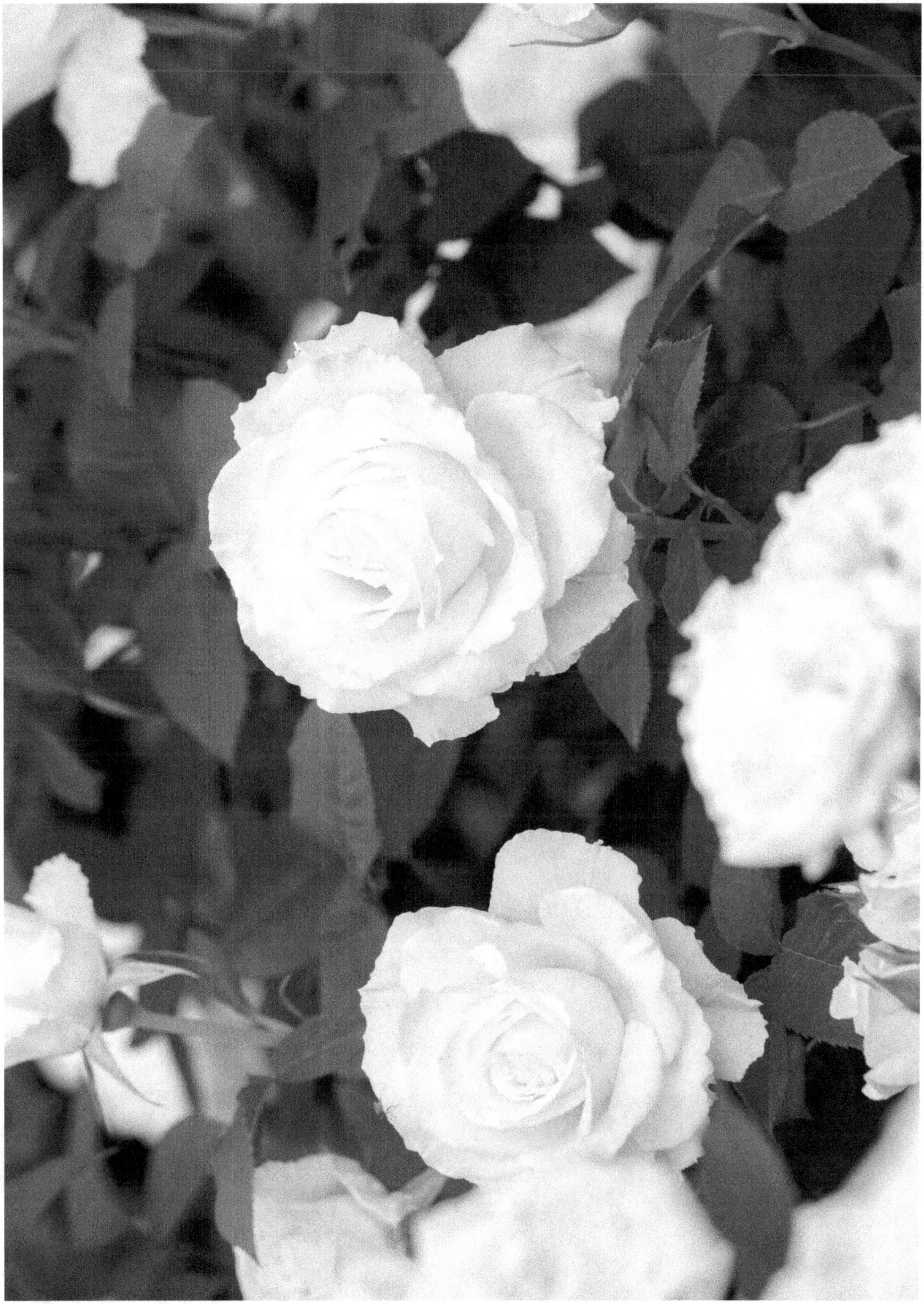

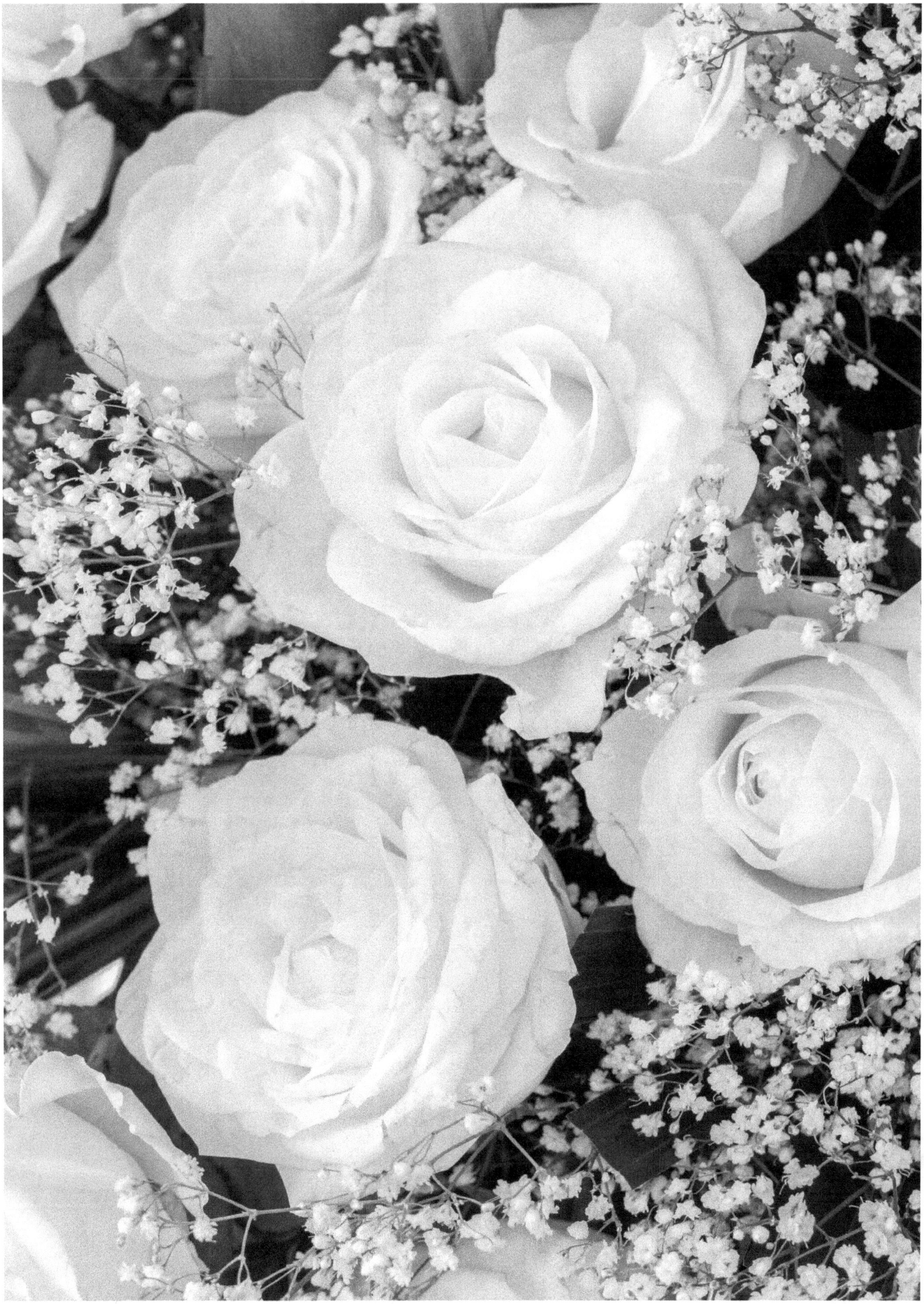

www.ingramcontent.com/pod-product-compliance
Lightning Source LLC
Chambersburg PA
CBHW062124220526
45471CB00010B/3872